Nasser Hussain is a lectur
in the UK. His poems are
quite loudly.

BOLDFACE

Nasser Hussain

Burning Eye

This edition published by Burning Eye Books 2014

www.burningeye.co.uk

@burningeye

Burning Eye Books
15 West Hill, Portishead, BS20 6LG

ISBN 978 1 90913 638 0

To Susan Holbrook, for planting good seeds.

Contents

Buy and Sell and Give and Take

Rhythms

Trivial Pursuits

1. GEOGRAPHY

2. ENTERTAINMENT

3. HISTORY

4. ARTS AND LITERATURE

Part I

Buy and Sell and Give and Take

spice cabinet

I was a number and three quarters
and small enough to fit
> in the big wooden spice cabinet
> under the chopping block
> in front of my mother's slacks

I'd hide among the clinking jars
reading
the lion the witch and the wardrobe
so fantastic, such ice white queens
among the cardamoms the papadams
the dry chilis crushed for everything
the cloves reserved for
coughing winter mornings

heard the supper preparing
the where is the egg mutter

a slim brown hand
anticipating the interruption
would fish out the nutmeg
and offer

breakfast

an old man with sunshine caught between his teeth
drooling good mornings
asks for more coffee

a signpost on your daily paper route
read it eaten forget it and gone
move on

the most important sneer of the day
ham and egg ham and egg and hams and eggs
scram ham sand eggs man damned daily sad papers

> truth a   hot grill   a spatula
> white memory   handle sticky
> with flame   pure as pain
> burns hurt now   no laters

for the waiters out of serviettes and patience
all things being equal to the
bacon skaters on lumberjack griddles
adam and eve on a raft writing riddles
greasy and rhyming, I stop trying

and recall

ham sand egg soar easy burnt oats on the side
and I'm eight minutes into taking five
while the egg sand hammers pound another
cholesterol nail down

more coffee please
more coif sheep leads
more cough lotion reliefs
a brief cheese dream omelette
and I rise
flap sleep from pancake eyes
        this is
        breakfast time

railsplitter

bent back
train tracks
skin black
trace that
sweat stain
      bead

sounds

a sound is

a pound of blue

a pond you

would swim

across

strokes like sable

brushes

tickling

your inner

matisse, or

ear.

business speak

I'm so close to the means of my production I can smell it. coffee tastes a bit like sweat. the lucid limit of my language. the plastic limit of my overdraft. da doo doo doo, da da da da, that's all I want to scat at you. they call it scat for a reason, but there is no reckoning three hours into a meeting, between floors, or buckled in for the takeoff. my ass is the means of my morning production. the relief of everything I eat. all labour runs to scat. all bacon strips in the end. chit-chat about cat shit. a ruined duvet and the effort to care. pain is a vertical index of humour. the more it hurts, the more we laugh, slapsticks in unison. groins tighten in dark theatres. a piece of work can't get much closer than that. if it looks like a hershey kiss, walks like a hershey kiss, talks like a hershey kiss, don't trust it my friend. I said *don't trust it* because you are my friend even though I don't like you. the best way to make friends is to make friendly. the leeward calmer seemingly. but the wind is the collected farts of a ruminate planet, and it's easy to confuse a new idea with breaking wind. in elevators especially. it wasn't me, I'm thinking, and you know it's true since I am the friendly sort. I quit producing before I came to work this morning, so it couldn't be.

consumer, meet enema (for Rob)

yes I want to
receive sales information

oh yes I want to receive sales
information
so yes I

want to receive sales information

I want

sales information
by email
by text message
by pony express
by by bye
(the way some people say 'bye-eeee')
is this connection slow?
by now, I'd have the slaes informatino
er, the sleas information:

take my PIN take my security number take my details
(you're not just dealing with me but everyone in my search history)

five-star rating, would do business again and again and
again until we are more than just paypals, but friends.

bark odes, last day,
    everything must
go.

smoking

the basso lung oyster
the shaker of rooms, boom
here comes the choke victim
have you seen him
check the size of his cilia
bending, a palm frond on a so named beach

rehearsing a death rattle
breathe a new battle
hauling ass
up stairs
he don't need to knock no more

lord don't let me get that sick
lord I'll be good and clean and quick
if you don't let me get dead
lord be my oxygen tank instead
lord tracheotomy, honestly
I don't wanna be hobbled by the atmosphere
I don't need a new lump here.
I want to pick plums from the stumps
of a lung orchard at a full run

my ashtray full of guilty
cigarettes, twelve calendars
rolled up and lit
my clothes smell like shit
bits of dried leaf

an addiction-seeking missile

book

leafing along,
you gasp.
afterword,
all you long
for is another
introduction.
such touches

worm

no one tells the worm
that today
will be the day.

the worm will just be there
the shovel will just come down
the shovel will just be there
like the worm is just there
like the rock in front of the worm is just
there.

there is no worm calendar to warn.
there is no annelid calculus to predict.

the shovel will just descend
and that will be that .

the worm, exposed,
a squirming lip
on a chocolate cake,

will not know today was the day,
but will instantly tense,
an entire body's soft might
thrusting down with an untapped speed.

today,
without apologies,
the gardener hums the song
stuck in his head.

executional excellence

don't just 'win win',
win win *win*!
we e-commerce solutions for licensing poets who
trickle down into manageable chunks, so let's
position product and bucket
strategically so we can
turn data into information into knowledge into insight.

(analyze around the gap to engender actionable forecasts, dude.)

we implement appropriate metrics and accountability for leading
    and lagging
indicators that will track progress
against the strat plan.

(win win win win?
ain't that a tie?)

drive the project ramping down the operation,
put it in the parking lot, and

regardez – rising tides raise all boats!

issue is problem, and value is added,

then the iteration of corporate culture
will engineer passback to shareholders
who
prize granularity of cash burn rate
while we
practise ambush marketing.

if results drive the brand soul,
spin it!
and don't drop the ball on the 360
feedback loop.
question with clarity and trim the fat.

(win win win win win)

I'm resonating with aha.

if the juice is worth the squeeze, say please,
or look up:

highly successful people or something.

glow

I was eight. shoved it under my shirt, tucked my head under the collar. summoning the dark. under my parents' bed, inside the washing machine, in the big brown suitcase, the light, devious, serpentine, liquid, still found me. at dusk, stuffed into my closet, I opened my palm, waited for a miracle. shades of nuclear fallout, glowing in my hand. creases in my palm. read under the covers. why isn't everything made of this stuff? here, the potential to keep the night at bay forever. in this gamma-ray nimbus, industrial applications. print books on it; draw lines through the hallways and the kitchen for a glass of water. or to the bathroom for a midnight pee. paint the toilet bowl with it. wear a shirt of the stuff, never argue over going to bed early. worldly possessions would gently turn a mellow green and irradiate my room as the sun set. eat dance and play in the dark. I'd never lose anything that was *mine*. I could never lose my way.

language is the engine of humour

a banana peels because it's funny. peel a word, you might find fruit. peel a banana and find a symbol, just trying to be sweet. can foucault please explain why we spank each other for fun? I discipline my puns impishly. no one is naughty when roleplaying. or occupying a new subject position. there is an agenda afoot. gendering my foot. sexing my walk. fucking my gait. lying down is the ultimate capitulation. obelisk capitalist. what makes a pyramid strong? rendering geometry into literature is risky. now that's a word. there is a humorous hegemony afoot. keep your bananas to yourself, discard the peels, and await the slip, the hijinks, the laugh track derailing a coherent train of thought every five seconds. laugh along. stop when the sign tells you. start again when the sign stops being stop. where does an octagon say temporarily? all it takes to go is a breath. magic when someone waves you in and tells you to go even though you can't hear him. go ahead in spite of the euclid of it all. standing in the middle of the road to beat the yellow. lights come in cereal box colours. look before crossing the sign. why did the chicken transgress foucault? to get the grecian urn.

glass

this is intimate
the smooth run
of tongue over
the lip, the ridge,
the saxophone
of a drink.
all the intoxication
is an afterthought

satellite

lay down with the satellite
where's the remote
channel flicker
coffee's black
the image thinner

yes honey, I'm listening
this sunday
the christening
no missing
I'm listening

please cheapen
my lover
I'm sweeter than lower
my equal
my only
tabs fizzing
images dwindling
I'm lonely

Gilligan! sweet skipper
so ginger
the nipple
remote flickers

yes honey, I'm listening
discoveries bristling
teeth whitening
muscle relaxing
lazy boy ears

solo like black coffee
where's the double
double
cleansing bubbles
troubled women
break the huddle

yes honey, I'm whistling
Chanel numbers glistening
cat walks quickening
remote channels flickering
image dwindling

please, lover, cheapen
sweetly, lower, breathe, in

my equal so only
my body exploding
tab is fizzing
belly dieting
images flickering
satellites nippling
prime times conflicting

yes honey, I'm listening.

vengeance stood before me in a line

skull   cap and a half

subheading:

                   bad ass
                   sweetback

nervous wallets
twitching for the
forward pass:

it
may flower, may even score

police mean
history

a sister, carrying concealed opinions—

a new, literal
                  folder.

month

twenty-eight butterflies
baked in a pie.
left on the sill
for forty-eight hours
until a thumb-thick
high jumper
stuck it in the fire.

abstract egypt

tis is this after several revolutions
this uppity typing
and a refusal to say that this is is
isis
osiris
iris
seeing the dead return
reseeing the rerun
a simpsons
as imps on esses slide down

        a pole

        or

        an

        i

tsk, tsk, ma cherie
I told you before
I have no sis
only this is purple or risible

half of one, six dozen of the other

you wash the brush, the brush washes you
self-esteem is the highest tautology
fifty percent of statistics are improvisations
a train is a raincoat at top volume
hammers made the world harder
design assign resign

what I do on lunch breaks

holy sexual

refuses to
enter discourse
or
     that course
for that matter.

love is in
lungs lunges urges and lunches
                    I eat

note on my door:
              gone burgeoning—
                   —back later

movie night

take out a stain and you got a clean shirt for thursday
teach them to do laundry and your ironing is done forever

someone paints lampposts for money
the ones in my neighbourhood are green

I never heard of a poem like this before

as usual, nothing is planned in advance
this is a line to trip over. I need those

topographic maps for the honeymoon
the hills have lines where I'm going.

lost my boot in a snowbank when I was
six and passive aggressive. I monkeyed

with the tin tan bathroom scale, dialled
the springs to maximum tension, and

pretended a ten-pound me. I was good
on the moon.

attack the world with as much wit as
you can muster, and take a hot dog for later

I was an ass man, now I'm undecided

the nominal is not limiting
mug is as good as glass

the world is almost the world

always an ell short, or
a fur long. short linguist,

the inventor, dreams of
unique conventions, combinations, not

necessarily originality. galileo
was a lying leo for a reason

morning noon and night morning
noon and night they yelled titanics

through walls, pillows floors doors
blood in the chilis makes them hotter

no daughters, but two girls.
people are conspicuously absent

from books. leave that
stack industrial. I never figured

out which fence s/he straddled

dismantled factories produce ironic
splits. the ice cream scoops are

square there. a sharp wire
almost took my wife's hand.

she speaks yoga when
she comes. Forefingers

curled to thumbs, three
remain splayed in a wide

meditation. thirty seconds
of kripalu remind me of

a hometown girl and
limber cartwheels. I sprain

easily. you never think of
toes unless you break or have

a fetish. nothing more
ambiguous than a

sign. direct sunlight
blinds and sustains

hard canonical shell
creamy idea filling

inches off your landfill
get cut. a ripped landscape.

build a graceful windmill
with a book stolen from

the library. I could salt
the earth with them and who

would notice? hypnotised
by phrases in mathbooks,

I chord the circle. diameter
defeats me especially. the

most important angel sows
dandruff: value added products

aren't so different from

contradictory presidents. I deny
my past. where is my ulna again?

wanted a pun and ended up
with people. a white line is worth

a change of subject

position. the pen's smitier
(as in smites more and harder)

than the word. no, no,
you're not interrupting.

a caress without curves
is quite kinky. no errors

with telephone operators.
dial. soap smells.

everybody hurts in athens,
georgia. NO, I said, I'm not

angry, just suffering random
juts in the guts. I shave penitent

shower to shower to stinging to
singing to after shave tomorrow.

it's worth fifteen percent. a girl
named after a muslim mount

made a mixed tape of my
formative years. more form

to come. film at eleven.
they told me you can't

spend what you don't
have. I refer them to

a poem I read in 2003.

all I howl is watered down
blues. latin is dead in south

america. take more photos.
side arm pitcher of lemonade

bricolage is the secret handshake
for our intellectual masons. But

I am not conspiracy minded, fellow.
there's no good way to end a line with

israelites. there's no good ending
when the oxygen line breaks and

bond james bond has a harpoon
in his pants. some body floats

away, dies off camera.

soyworld©

a whole new set
of excellent activists
predict the bend

and now I'm intolerant?

soy joy
    sells
    sex
    nog

soy suns set
    nicely
soy thinks

soy toys
    pants
    gasm
    free

don't soy me
wrong, I been here
beef or

I cut skins
open, pulped
flesh, salted
ears

gemmed my ohs but good I did

oleo
oleo

soy my soul clean
in case nothing grows

whaler

—well, I was at the bar like all night, and finally the landlord gave me a bed since it was so late and there was nowhere else to go, and he tucked me in like my grandmother used to when I was really little, and just before I got to sleep this big scary man came into the room and undressed and jumped into the bed, and even though he had the most wicked tats, I called the landlord, and he made everything savvy, and then I got back into the bed with the tattooed man, and I never slept better in my life, you know, and next thing I know, I wake up with his arm over me, and he's treating me like we're married or something, and I just decide to go with it, and he's wearing his best tux, top hat 'n' tails, and we go out on the town and I'm just, like, hanging off his arm until we end up at this place that serves, like, the best chowder you EVER HAD, and we get home really late, and I guess we got serious after that.

we both found jobs at the same place, and things got complicated. we just kept talking shop at nights, and even though I was just in the secretarial pool, I knew what was going on in the boardrooms – everyone talked about it in the canteen and out on the floor. one day the boss came in and got all drunk and started shouting about baptisms and revenge and how he had contracted some work out to the iranis even though we could do the job just as well and some stuff about fate and conspiracies and then he nailed one big bonus to the board, and told everyone how it wasn't about the oil at all, but we all knew that everyone was going to go down soon, like in three days' time.

I don't see my tattooed fella anymore, but that was a really good weekend.

right back at you ee

my father was   never

which isn't to say

              he wasn't

just that
              he didn't

and I probably   was.

& even   though
I know
              I shouldn't,

I do.

wing chun

two feet
walks on

one foot
hops

no feet
crawls

but

knows
this much

two feet
stands firm

no feet
knows loss

but one
foot one
foot

always
falls

skin

start with the fingerprint
follow that panoptical aid to its conclusion
end up on the back of the finger where it mischievously dissipates
    into anonymity
(why don't criminals use the backs of their hands)
and it becomes a wave that cascades
into the tiny wrinkles of the first joint
too soft to be a knuckle
the white bread of a violent
sandwich from there to the second joint
the beginning of a shut up
the inconclusive circles of silence
up to the second history of gripping
flowing into the follicles of fine hairs
little islands of primate
too short to drag
grind against the ground
flat plane of a punch
into the web again knowing
no one else is marked thus
a million stretches
a billion popping noises
worn like boots
inevitable evidence of the effort
that no matter what I hold on to
I need you
you old proteus

thank you

thank you god
for this knife in my back

you're really keeping me on my toes

blades of grass
and no handles
the tang of dew
on my lizard
tongue. halved
brains
scrotum
mitochondria

a long razor
machine-made
just for all occasions

energy is for expenditure
expenditure is for change
and change is for good

god of static cling
god of jingles
god of cherry pits
all hollowed out and affordable
god of stumbles and staircases
what else could be made
in taiwan
these manicured lawns
haunted by our dry garden
hoses, abandoned tractors

now our ploughshares
are beaten back
change is a fact
but regress is a flank attack
history from way back
may appear closer
in a rear-view mirror

and this god is a serial killer

and we're working
the most mysterious case ever
he ain't gonna stop
until
he's got us all

this is not a moral place
this is not a comfy chair

absolutions and thigh masters

no, god,
I don't blame you

I just hoped
it would be sharper

marriage is not ending

you live in the same world I do. so let's kill crows with rocks. if you will. if you won't it won't as it is wont to do. you live in the same world I do. so do two birds twittering, too. singing on my doorstep. signing on my newsprint. a bee pees somehow. and it can fly. you can be up or down. this is the same as trying to be two. this is a powerful comma. come on, you don't expect me to believe this insistence is the same as intensification. no. that is precisely the point. a precis of a pointed critique. they lived in the same world I live in. they insist on living. but you are a life. you are alive. this is the same world as a minute. tastes like a second. helping. this is the powerful period. you are alive in the same world I do. I do the world too. as you do. I like it. I do.

outside the box

what if the government spent its military budget on restoring
    classic cars
what if snails were money
what blackboards and whiteboards and smartboards were
    segregated
what if time really were money
if you could weigh a photon
what if you could lose weight fast
what if you could really grow your penis four inches
what if you could get ripped
and what if ripping four inches was how to lose weight fast
that guy in nigeria really did want to buy your used camera and
    was willing to pay extra for it
that guy in nigeria really did have twenty million dollars in an
    account that he needed to get out of
the country fast because his uncle was being pursued by a mad
    dictator and you could get a
twenty percent cut of the proceeds

permanent markers really were permanent
there were no more internet
the oil actually ran out, and you had the last bucket
we've already seen the apex of our civilisation
what if we're still evolving – could you determine this with a
    thorough examination of your facebook
friends
enough has already been written about life on the lower east side
all the walls were made of paper
all the floors were made of sponges saturated with ink

this were a story and not a poem

someone already did this and called it sunset debris or someone
    else came along and like a
smart aleck fed it to an internet chat-bot called alice and wrote
    down everything that it said and
called that poem busted sirens

what if you read this

rough drafts were all you got
and that advice your father gave you about measuring twice and
    cutting once had no application in your life
our education system produced a generation of cut-'n'-paste
    wizards that could make anything look
original

you were conservative in conversation but liberal with lunchmeat

you couldn't give up just yet
I weren't here
gravity were on a pay-as-you-go basis
what if we cracked the code
hallmarks were the only thing you could write about in a
    Hallmark card
nobody invented yeast
your password were password
you wrote something and posted it online and people responded
    to it based on your race
what if your profile picture were a landscape

Dvorak and Betamax and DeLorean had proved successful

what if you had to make everything you owned
you had to waste everyone you knew

you had to trace everything you thought
return everything you bought
had to home a scared crow
had to eat a sacred cow
had to decide right now

had to pick a plan based on your usefulness and not your usage
had an exit strategy
had a hammer
had to hammer
had to move tomorrow
had to stare at a goat
had to bury a hatchet and had no shovel
had to call it home
what if you had to have a nap
had to have a map
had to hang out
had to hang up
had to hang ten
had two heads and two hangovers
had to read all of this and ask the question
had to eat cereal for political reasons and watch
news for breakfast

what if language were everything
if all there was *was* language
if verbs cost money
if you had more than bill gates
if you had to bill bill gates
if you had to gate bill gates
if you had to gate bill gates and bill bill gates for that gate
if you had to live on the bill that you gave bill gates for his new

gate

if it were a scandal: bill gates in billgatesgatebillgate

what if you had to think outside the box

if the box were the size of the room

the house

the tent

the countryside

the nation

the planet

the galaxy

the known universe

the unknown universe

what if the box were a horizon

what if you reconciled the very large and the very small

if superlatives weren't enough to express the largeness the
    smallness

if you had to resort to measurement

technical jargon

nano meso femto

mega giga bigga

what if imagination weren't enough

if you had to work

if this were my JOB

what if it's all economic

if marketing were an evolutionary advantage

if nature were ergonomic

if moths sold silk

if caterpillars unionised

if beavers pelted if rabbits skinned

if olives pressed

if cows milked
if sheep milled
what if it really were butter?
if it really were new and improved
if raspberry were blue

what if pubs served toads we could lick for a night's entertainment
then you could order a toad for the road
and complain on monday morn that you had one toad too many
     that you'll never toad again but for
lunch you'd shrug and order one claiming that the best cure is a
     lick of the toad that bit you and
toad in the hole would take on an entirely new and deviant and
     sexualised meaning – getting toed in the rump would replace a
     good asskicking and mr toad would become a counterculture
     hero a lovable rogue with a paper and smoking a fag a symbol
     of why everybody must get toad

what if they run out of comic books to turn into movies
run out of TV shows to remake (there was an old lady who lived
     in a reboot)
what if everything that came after post-modernism were to be
     characterised by a healthy scepticism
about remastered narratives

what if YOU were reading THIS
if I could imitate YOUR voice perfectly would it be the same or is
     there some part of you that can't
be reproduced

what if you lived in your body

Part II

Rhythms

they say change is good for you

so today you don't pop two you pop three
and maybe now you see that your desk
isn't an anchor but a tree and its branches spread out
and underneath, you're completely dry and shielded from them
    UV rays
and it strikes you that you haven't been to that club since last day
you know the one where the dj sharpens his needles and double-
    clicks the junglee switch
and the dancefloor skips to the beat of your own personal trip
and you hip hop on out onto the breeze that insinuates itself
    between you and your shirtsleeves
take a drag of pure ease

and when the man on the street says 'please'
you reach into your too-skinny jeans and find the change he's
    pleading for
and you dig in deeper and find there's more, and more so you
    treat yourself to a
coffee and a copy of *leaves of grass*
and you sing the body internet, you place your bet against death
    and you win a golden pen that's sharp as a pin
and you ask for a glass of writer's block and the girl at the counter
    stops you from looking at anything

and you see, you see fundamentally
the starry yin-yang tattoo on her left breast, and all the flakes of
    metal in her face
and you wonder at how long it musta took for her earlobes to
    learn to take up so much space
and you trace your finger round the latte stain
and you look at whitman dead in the grave and you learn to fall

like rain in autumn
or you learn to autumn like rain in fall
and you stall a bit, and make a note,
and the note's about truth and you're still thinking about the
    counter girl in you
and you wonder if she left any place on her body whole and true
and whitman's outside looking at betelgeuse or stalking goose and
    for the first time in history the person on your left's horoscope
    was precisely true and right – cuz tonight's the night she's
    gonna meet a tall and dark and handsome fight –
and the counter girl asks if you're finally through

you look up

she smiles
you squint

and she says: change is good for you

where I'm from

so, uh, where do you come from?

i come from my mum.

a duh adumb.
shoulda saw that one come from a mile and some.

so where's yer mum from?

ah, good question, my dear chum, let's entertain a theory or some:
perhaps my mum's from some slum –
an alum from the school of tough bumps and got none,
slung half her life on just one
papadam till someone saw how she stunned
the panjandrum with her bum-bum,
and took her straight to number one.

or, umm,

maybe my mum is from money like oildrums.
got ten maids with twenty thumbs;
so as far as lifting her fingers went,
count 'none' – and they went numb
from a thousand and one nights of no one
usin' 'em, so she flexed them by abusin'
her forty sons, one of which got it in his turban
to run to the land of opportunism,
heard the rumours of Americans:

> come one, come tons, bring your bad lungs your bleeding
> gums your misshaped huns your lumps and bumps and

hungered shunned to my shores and we can all live as cousins
in one unbroken gun-bumpin' bible-thumpin' publicly funded
tax-evading haven from them dumb Britons.

oh pardonne – I'm just having fun. don't want to offend anyone.

but you want to know where I'm from, englishman?

I'm from islington but
the blood of a brahmin
thuds in my cerebellum.

I come from that gathering of huts,
a ka-na-ta among the algonquin shrubs

I'm from bethlehum, islamadum, boom-a-bad, and bangleterre.
I'm from west of the sun, south of the moon, east of your ear, and
    ober dere.

I'm from the corner of elm and sesame street

I'm from the app store on iTunes like a download: I'm free

I came fresh from the veg stand
and I brought. you. these. beets.

I come from that luggage left all suspicious like.
I come from a Brazilian plumber's house who wishes you got it
    right.
I come straight off the canvas after a cassius clay fight.

and you're not the first to ask which is why I'm so various.
apparently the most interesting thing about me is my provenance.
what is it about me that makes me so alien? is it my accent, my

airs, or my aggressive
behaviours?

'cause the truth is:

I come from a very long line of humans

from the initial oozes right up to the present confusions.
I come from the womb, the same one you sprung from,
and that, son,
should be remarkable enough.

the thing

the thing about alien is the tripe
the thing about stomachs is the flex
the thing about arnie is the accent
the thing about language is the rest
the thing about sleep is the position
the thing about grids is the cross
the thing about jesus is the carpentry
the thing about chests is the breasts
the thing about gender is the binary
the thing about code is the rendering
the thing about fat is it's ugly
the thing about art is he's fat
the thing about meteorites is the chance of it all
the thing about bingo is futility
the thing about beckett is timing
the thing about comedy is distance
the thing about roads is cargo
the thing about weight is gravity
the thing about wrinkles is ironing
the thing about laundry is quarters
the thing about fractions is usefulness
the thing about school is it's not
the thing about spiderwebs is spider poo
the thing about babies is baby poo
the thing about families is financial
the thing about money is love.

motto

I'm not left-wing,
I'm left over,
the guts that
don't get into
mink stoles, or
garage sale
failures of
character.

I'm not paranoid,
just postmodern
fragments of
special effects
simulacra
(voice over).

I'm not resisting.
no really, I insist.
just frictioning
like any good
particle
pass over.

I'm not repeating,
not repeating.
in spite of some
setbacks, we re-
record the
old tapes, hear
old stories:

the best minds beaten
in with nightstick
politics. a lost layer
of soil means less petrol
for later. running
things honourably
in absentia. sex, hugs, proxy
and roll. windows,
aluminium and siding.
moose display, horses
are for riding. praxis
express. see them,
with earphones on the
frontlines. unconfirmed
rumours, near the old
valley. the pony is
coming. the vision is reality.
you can be surprisingly
literate on the couch

what a good thing to keep in mind.

timely, accurate and
thoughtful. you can
depend on me. experienced,
hard-working and
unquestioning. what
grandfathers knew is
made oil by time.

I'm not arguing,

I'm agreeing.
oh no, I know
what you mean
when you say
that was is
what is was.

we vague all
day, a dance
without brains
under a sky
we made
of desperation.

hailing

you who poll votes
you who pool views
you who stole oil
you who sing tang
you who bring thing
you who where as
you who that which
you who know those
you who war far
you who near past
you who fear rue
you who row fast
you who find this
you who fist tines
you who first time
you who smell gas
you who bull doors
you who dull boors
you who pill heads
you who skulk chores
you who chant storm
you who shit chat
you who fill form
you who can't, wait
you who be born
you who birth babes
you who same them
you who gave great
you who choose chance
you who blind faith

you who fruit peel
you who pain taste
you who plain feel
you who pop cans
you who plait waists
you who can do
you who teach learn
you who spies dark
you who pot ferns
you who read books
you who tread bare
you who slip feet

jazzwork

what's up bubble?
you wanna ruble?
I got no scruples
I'll rumble ten goebbels
so scramble, goobers
stumble rivers
eject the supers
my crew got new shoes
to kick loose
the booze, I can't
use fluids, I need food
gotta squeeze the sweat
shop out my George Foreman
grill
still,
there's so much dead labour to savour
while these machines pick my busy teeth clean
of strewn bones, ribosomes
solo lone tones
from a saxophone blown
forty years ago
lord knows I stole the soul
out ma bell's telephone
Monopoly boards, dissonant chords
a park place and a rusty Ford
the car was coveted by all.
groan loud, jones
me metatarsals splint
me maxillaries grin
spit lick and grind

these giant bones
flying is less form
than aviation
a pure state of mind
is worth more than a united nation
and to the left
diego rivera's a christ larger than death
all the new war heads need to get checked
cuz I'm poor, broke, and dissident
with nothing left but a breath
hanging out the neck

blaring american

u s a
u s a
you are us
u s a

I wanna be american
like

    charles ingalls hitting a grand slam
    breakfast and frisk down at denny's
    lenny bruce is screaming paki nigger
    a grove of freshly squeezed florida orange jews

    where curious kids with guns
    and curiously twisted white sheets
    drive houses with white fences and
    whitewall tyres
    defending dogs with deadly white teeth

    forgive me father for I have sinned
    gimme twenty to one that the dodgers win

    ok, corral
    and Special K the chuck wagons
    it's those damn no smoking signs
    that killed all the dragons

    and nobody dies in advertising
    lies masquerade as savvy strategising
    stomping down history
    like invading aboriginals
    no sense in stoppin' till you've
    carved your own memorial

american like that
u s a
u s a

baseball

high got the swing
high got the stride
hi de hi, hi de ho

low so below
low got broke
low de la low de lie

high so high
he popcorn below
sweet cherry pop
sweet cherry blow

low neck swing
red neck swung
low stop song
before sing begin

high swung sixty-one
sung seventy-two
low catch a bat
low strikeout, too

low know no joy
high play de ploy
high got the ride
low got the toy

sigh, games play
so slow for boys.

I don't speak no greek

eros rose sore this morn

zeus uses ruses to bazooka big bazongas boom boom boom

apollo allows solar solos

aphrodite is too difficult

psyche sighs ink, likely

ares all arse and marsh farts

boreas or lord blow

persephone's phone fits purse. say: funny funny

ariadne an abacus adding arachnids

dionysus, I die: wild iodine

athena a then a the ahem then at he

artemis nemesis deliciousness

poseidon poisoned poise. propose portions: purposes per porpoise

orpheus phones o'er us.

serious problem

you got a serious problem
you got a surrealist problem
you got a satellite television and
you gotta keep running david
you gotta keep running david hasselhoff.

the beach is deeper than pamela's tabloid tanlines
and you could just as easily be a stay at home kind of dad
with some bratty kid who wishes he had the kit you did

so keep running david
keep running david hasselhoff

cuz 23 brother snorting air
jordans
are gonna chase you offa this glass building

so slick you can lick a drink offa it,
see your face in it, chewing cheeseburgs on youtube

so keep running david
keep running david hasselhoff

make a jump cut a blade trim a waist
and land safe in sanitary garbage
no needles to prick that blue blue eye
don't touch that dial
and

keep running david hasselhoff

do something

do you know what
they been feeding us

do you know

they been feeding us
lines,
man
baloney sandwich
thick lines

what we gonna do

somebody gotta do something

gotta gotta
gotta make a pop record
gotta stop hip hop
and drop a lot of meatloaf
some engelbert humperdinck
some weak tea and milquetoast

somebody gotta do something

papa gotta brand new prop
papa gotta all new Pontiac

shock troops of hot sitcom
activists shop for war toys
at FAO Schwartzkopf

watch 'em lop the tops off
the GI Joes and burn down

Barbie's pantyhose wardrobe

somebody gotta do something

don't just sit on your laptops –
surf!

don't just browse –
order now!

we gotta do something
the time is prime

screaming in HD 3D TVs
goddamn painting giving me
the edvard munchies

shot put the pot pipe
and pirate gil scott CDs

somebody gotta do something
somebody gotta get them

a long distance plan
a sneeze guard attack

Dettol angels –
beneficent toilets

can't wait until then

somebody gotta short putt
that bill payment
slam dunk that legislation

slapshot that deficit

somebody gotta make that
stick and stick and stick
till it don't come out without
OxiClean or elbow grease

somebody gotta write a new line
a faster food line
a slicker byline
use your head line

somebody gotta do something

my speak

is whole block   bigger than brooklyn   used to the speech till I caught up with my self   quick tennessee like ginger bread from a wolf mouth   vocab like monkey see monkey what monkey see monkey what like that edge I got   pushed against so close a needle in your ear a needle in your arm   and flavour is a warning that time is on a chain   that is on a neck   and it's just too damn big and heavy bigger than brooklyn sometimes I   rhyme slow sometimes I run quick   I just keep running away   just keep running away   in   my Adidas   forget the laces I had enough of tying things up   it's time to break it down   so walk this way   walk this way   hit it run   doo wap shoo wap   doo wap shoo wap   do dat do disc to diss emma p three two one time broken glass in my apartment   now the street is   one time   too close and so far   ladies first   an' I dodge the needle as it washes up upon a sandy shore   on saturday it's a saturday it's a saturday y'all jump like it's brooklyn sized   one arm up like a lady inna harbour   skyscrapers and everything   I speak very fluent brooklyn you know like borough and bodega you know what I'm saying knowwhatI'msayinyo   pro pop locks and break dance on backs smooth like linoleum   supposing it's another jedi mind trick a black eye anna white stick   a crosswalk anna boy scout   who counts cars wishing he could go far on engine engine number nine on the new york transit line you so sweet and you so fine you done nearly stole my mind around the way my baby got base and a treble is a terrible thing to waste forget the house I'm in your place and out the back door left channels I break beats you leave hairline fractures   my speak captures like south african coppers catch kaffirs bigger than ten mandelas on five podiums eighteen arenas and a brownstone short of a building my speak is whole block

dancing in churches

I might not be right
but I am convincing.
I'm not urgent,
but I am pressing
up against your
mental furniture
suggestively. but just
when you do the dirty
dance (react) I pull pure
words from a can of
milk, nice and clean,
nice and clean, so true
so new, that you know
what I mean, know what
I mean? so trite you
nod in amen. some look
on, some look in, scrubbing
circles on frosty clichés,
windowpanes, and then I
can't decide which is worse,
dickens or church, a dearth
of bursting hip huggers
on earth. so I look out
and look up, a way
unsure, a dependable
erasure, a saviour for
rock and roll on every
corner, a Savion Glover
tapdancing lover, and
we all call alleluia, alleluia, alleluia

from concept to coltrane

rhyme is palimpsest
the echo and invocation of its sonic sphere
it is here and it is song
there and long ago
and far a field
all balls and rolling blunders
make no mistake the break heralds
the angels we labour under and wonder over
lover of where eyes
and thighs
collide
students colluding about which allusion is most mellifluous
or just enough to this moment
a nickel speckle in a torrent
short wars and long-armed warrants
cops shock perps
tasers
cocked hammers spare power supplies for hair raisers
hands up and don't reach for it
no phone call for you
dial louie up from retirement
we bagged another ne'er do nothing
much less nothing well

hell is twenty bullets
for all the plastic in your wallet
and it's all a simple fallout
a paranoia of accountants
and a bunch of paper options
written on the skins of onions

one october hallowed evening
when the makeup and the artist
who prefers to live in boxes
built of bombs and economics
met in baghdad over breakfast
taking solace in the oil well
gonna run out any minute
so we might as well just finish
cuz my caddy needs a daddy
that can bring home all the bacon and the
strippers live on tipping
not a city in north china
area has got more syllables
than space, or mere, or final and
a breath is hopeful when it's taken
sexual if it is stolen
biological involuntary
obligatory or beholden
what you breathing mister biscuit?
while you're in the oven tanning
there's a slave in calico
head kerchief and backlash hanging
on your every single letter
anthologised by our pal norton
who knows that canons are more
suited to the problem of the sorting
and where am I with all my metre
that I pulled from my vain pounding
at the balls of all the umps
crouching calling strike three tiger?

rhythm is the problem and solution
(all together now)

language got more angles
than a greek theoretician
the great encyclopaedia is
full of entries to be written
if it's bitter then it's bitten
and you're too fine for
definition when all this rhythm
leads to kissing. it's just that art is always
missing —

(the long slow lick
the song's low kick
spit valve and blow
the pure bone tone that
the saxophone knows:

no solo is played
alone)

Part III

Trivial Pursuits

1. GEOGRAPHY

spanish

what's on television is what's on my plate. it's always
the same warmed over. sanded-down burrs of words are
official and official is a special condition of telling vision.
language makes acts and bodies rock like hey, pop. lock
of air, lock of -ness. a funny little pin, voodoo
chile. you can say it. you can say it twice.

greece

what men! what women! what water! what left-overs! this
country music makes me mad as a small banker without
'is notes. he could sing a cockney rhyme, or whatever
the barometer chose for him. there's a deep well, there.
hellenic or not, here I come – take that to the
republic and shove it. ruins burn, george burns, we burn.

venice

what roads can't move? where there's oak, there's ire – a
city collects kindling, calls it history, charges admission for it.
would could go up just as wood gross up and
you may or mayor not want to beat it, so
be it. just be it. don' know whatchu meanin' be
in. show me how funky, show me just right. that's
if you can even feel the beat, lighting up streets.
you wade, hip deep, an anthem in a language you
were fluent in once. a salad of verbiage we spent
feeding ourselves on in bland canal-side cafés, dry, for
the moment, but not for long. the island called, and
pigeons called. an old pillar stuck in the middle of
in the middle of   (a glitch? a binary plop in
the ocean of data? shouldn't we be more concerned, sir?)
piazza tales, white jackets, huge innuendoes, and the ivory, it's
san it eyes her. a pump or two is enough.
marco. polo. marco. polo. marco. polo. marco. polo. marco. polo.

utah

where the spirit can be created from bare whole thought
in a matter of a few books, or a vision.
the candle and the cards move us to the west
US use what you find, find you what use, that
is the truth and the underwear proves it. my great
great mother knew the good book in a biblical sense.
salt peter, saint shaker, good wood for building, and a
lake bottom upraised for all of us to see, admiringly.

belgium

which border do you mean to cross when leaving me?
country or county, coastal or coaster or continental divide that
hosted game shows for game show hosts, a meta loser,
the mullets and bad suits, total lack of fashion senses
battle for the attention of my irises between commercial breakages
of toilet tissue, antacids, food from wholesome sources, hand
    sanitised
waterloo closets. break: fast, serially, and consume all you lost.

pretoria

what came before toria. what happened after the long hill
is a lungful. mouth opens, then closes round my journal
the likes of which hasn't been seen since the old
capital sank. now, a period of late capital schism, last
of the t-shirts calling out for changes in how far
south we can send our liberty, measured out in tines.
africa a fracas, china a teacup, europe theirs and americas.

the titanic

what can't have a sequel gets a remake
ship, shap, shop, shep, shup
sank
in until there is only shell, hull, brrr, rust
a brown skull, a sea floor
night like a night
to
remember how we bobbed, once.

culture club

what now, toy
band? what,
did you really want to hurt me,
boy? by
george, this
spring has too many accessories
to season your
fame
with.

the lovin' spoonful

what do you do when you're done?
group things on a menu, and get
asked if
the steak and sauce are
musical together, tonight?
question:
do you think anyone cares if
you wrote what you
believe
in?
magic can pass through a tablecloth, too.

WC fields

who is born every minute,
said 'ayieee' in the east.
a simple tent deception.
woman, yes. there's no word better.
drove out in the rain to meet
me. there was a lot
to
drink
and
I
never drink.
had a manhattan. had an old-fashioned.
the grasshopper was a
courtesy.
to
thank
her, I took down the circus.

corporal klinger

who you can't be is the best disguise.
was it here? or tucked under?
the thing is best squeezed in plain sight.
transvestite operators
in suits sharper than surgeons.
mash shampoo: do your makeup in the shower.

a dead rat

what restaurant
did
bette run?
davis desserts, or is that just?
serve to love
up on a hanger
to two love
joan oh joan
crawford.
in your awful closet
whatever I know I learned from TV, and you
happened to be all over it:
to get out, then, you must go deeper
baby, temple, velvet, and
jane.

3. HISTORY

red

what the bloody hell
is the bloody problem
the bloody fellow said the bloody
colour
of the bloody sofa was bloody well in
the bloody
leather bloody hell
in blood. bloody well bloody cover
the bleeding walls of the bloody
house
of bloody
lords, why don't you?

menachem begin, jimmy carter, anwar sadat

what ever could have brought us here
three of us on a card
leaders builders and victims
signed what they put in front
the pen broke sometimes, but they never show that part
camp laughs, so typical
david slings, we free sing our hosannas and
accords.

winston churchill and franklin roosevelt

what comes, comes in the blood
british or not, here I colonise
prime for ruling, n'est pas?
minister banister
and
US hulkster (or
president ball buster)
were
seventh in line behind nine royal
cousins who
once flew to the bottom of the canyon and forcefully
removed the office from themselves.

the mau mau

what was fought for
was of no concern to the undergraduate.
the rumble of history just another
name to miss, pronounce.
of vodka and pot noodle, just ask
the price, and you get flawless research. of
african
independence, some
movement made in response to liberty and how nwoye is a tragic
    shakespearean
that can't see the hamlet in front of him, you get confusion.
    (instead they
fought the stereotype, grappled with
the imported nicknames and literary structures and the
british felt bad about it, really, but
in all honesty, and in conclusion, it kind of had to happen. at least
    way back in
kenya
in
the
1950s.)

the left

which switch did you pick
eye went for the thick stick
did she lick it quick
moshe tricked her with a big twitch
dayan night
wear what you like, she'll swing
a brick and you'll think her nice.
patch yer pants or it's poor punishment
over and outer.

the *times*

what paper is it in
did you forget
the joke about it
daily amnesia
universal completion rate, but then, what
register really registers?
become a bureaucracy
in your spare time at home, make
1788 a month.

4. Arts and Literature

american

what say can you see
nationality brand
was hardest smote by
the backhand of the
artist market in mothers and rocking?
james 'the whistler'
whistler is coming to the ring.

prostitute

what the sheen
is going down here?
the media is a greeting card, the scandal a
profession of faith made
of infidelity, caught in HD.
nursery school
rhyme teachers, or suchlike unsavoury
characters like
lucy lost her jewellery: a
locket of wheat,
and a
kitty diamond and a
fisher tiara.

love in a cold climate

what, what, what?
was it too much like a hot country?
nancy is dutch, wants her pancake
mitford's or mit slagroom or somesuch.
chilling in the crisper makes
love more like lettuce. that's all the
story you could, or should, want told.

jeeves

what does the internet *really* want? to be
famed out, chromed to the tits? its own
butler to ask it where it is?
did we trade it all for
PG Tips, and a biscuit? (half of britain knows a
woodhouse, but lives in a brick tip.)
create, and get ready to start your search engines, gentlemensch.

michelangelo

what the hell. I'm no
artist.
had a gimmick, though.
the first words weren't mine, any more than a
last
name is yours.
buonarroti knows.

son of

what went up your leg like a curious glance –
do you notice, or deflect with grace and body hair?
mc superman
and wonder
mac woman can get pretty
mean (ornery)
when they drink.
used to play a game, using the moon to carve
in their
surnames.

5. Science and Nature

AD 1

what else goes around the sun? a

year compared to a tock

followed by a tick –

1 then 0, a

BC the effigy. hi, jay kay. elle, mmm? no, peek you are street

(abbr): you've doubled

ewe, ex-wisely.

a grenade

what goes up must go boom
type 'boom' or style it, roy. hell's knells! some
of them are civil, if not innocent.
bomb etiquette, or call them foxhole converts, all it is
is a weak glue when it meets
a strong force.
mills grind them out: we're
bomb children.

gold

what fools you only makes you stranger.
are you tuned in, kenny? this is an
iron clad copy you can take to the white house.
pyrites: the mineral conceptual,
often correct, but never
mistaken
for the real thing is still out there.

panther

what's going down
another drain – a fancy
term for return, reverse, representation.
for a mule? hell. I'll take four more years of what he's having.
a good word, wrapped in a fist. and
black eyes all around, smoking: comfort for an old
leopard.

the uterus

what an unbelievable

organ. I

gave a talk about it in 1972: *You Into*

Us: the Word Makes Flesh Makes Word.

the men in the audience held their water until someone gave the

word, and no one used

hysterical ever again.

the brain

where are you in all these folds?
would you just clean your room without an argument for god's
    sake?
you know I mean allah, smartass.
find me that thing.
the thing, you know. the one that makes it go. the
medulla in the jar. sing! sing loud, igor: obladi, oblada,
oblongata.

the Rubik's Cube

what metaphor
was hid in this block of primaries?
1981's just 1198 or 1891 or 8911 or 9811 or 8191. the
best I could get was three sides. picking stickers, adhesive fingers,
selling books on how best to twist it. this was our idea of a
toy.

eddie kid

who knows how long a bus really is?
(provided you've never been late in london
england's spongy morning.)
answer the crowd for once, jump a double decker just
to get the doughnuts, forget about the fame – even in his name
evel
knievel made repetition heroic.

the US

whatever you do, your
country isn't *actually* behind you. even if you
won the battle of
the bulge, came in
first at church, gave all the
gold in china to tibet, wrested the
medal of honour from the president herself
in a POW camp in korea,
the fact is that
first thing in the
modern mind each
day is everything other than the
olympics.

technical knockout

what bambambam
does bambambam
TKO bambambam
stand (uh)
for.

a golf ball

what in the name of nicklaus
did just happen? the green
floyd, the
rose gardened
drive stretched
across the old plain.
the factory where it was, all
US fields, once.

martina navratilova

what made my birthday special. a
czechoslovakian national holiday.
tennis, but not cricket.
star but not idol.
defected is a word for correction
to the right reporter.
the spoils of sponsorship in the
US, tucked into a short skirt, no pockets
in there, just room for biceps, all
1975.

Acknowledgements

spice cabinet, glass, and **I don't speak no greek** were published in
Stand 12:1 (2013)

breakfast was published in *Jones Av.* (Toronto, 2001)

consumer, meet enema was published in *Detours: An Anthology*
(Palimpsest Press, Kitchener, Ontario, 2013)

movie night was published in *Poetry and Audience* (Leeds
University, 2008, ISSN: 00322040)

outside the box appeared in *The Windsor Review* in 2013

The **Geography** section of **Part III: Trivial Pursuits** has appeared
among the works in the online collective:
myfatherlostmetothebeastatcards.wordpress.com (2012)